THE ART OF FOLDING

Sarah Zale

Plain View Press
P. O. 42255
Austin, TX 78704

plainviewpress.net
sb@plainviewpress.net
512-441-2452

Cover Photo by Louise LeGresley, "Paper Crane By Window"

Acknowledgements

I am grateful to the delegation of compassionate listeners
I traveled with to Israel and Palestine in November
2006—especially to our guides, Leah Green and Maha El-Taji,
who helped us understand violence as wound.

My thanks to Michael, Sam, and Joey, the first to hear these
poems; to Sam Hamill, Carolyn Forché, Heather K. Hummel,
and Martha Silano for their comments. Deep gratitude to Juliana
Spahr and Truong Tran for their inspiration and support.

My appreciation to the editors where these poems first appeared:
"An olive hard and dark, hiding," "My love does not see the
violence," "The leaves blink like brushed silver," "Reuven looks
to the lone tree on the hill," "The bread still too warm to slice,
we," *Arabesques Review: International Poetry & Literature*, 2007;
"Well past fifty, I shed my first tear," "Anita of Brooklyn heard
the call—aliyah!" "The tide of fealty ebbs," *Quay Journal of
the Arts*, 2007; "I remember my mother" (pub. as "Laundry"),
Comstock Review, 2008-9; "I feel ironed, says Rose" (pub. as
"Dance With Me"), *Her Mark: Woman Made Gallery*, 2009;
"Aman understands the walnut" (pub. as "The Folly of Half"),
Come Together, *Imagine Peace Anthology* (Bottom Dog Press),
2009.

سلام
שלום

I thought one day I would find answers
in the press of my hands.

Beyond moan and wound as I counted stars
through the arched wall of glass at a train station,
I would remember the dead. I would understand paper—
hemp and kozo. Mulberry. We would fold crane
after crane, and talk—the first time—about war.

I would give up drinking
with those who knew all the lines
from my movie. I would live in Camelot,
hold a light. Ships of tired and huddled masses
would sail to my door.

People would call me Emma, call me Ruth,
call me Esther. They would say Rose, you are Rose,
you are whole, you are holy. Every Rose is a rose is a rose.

Mark the first page of the book with a red marker. For, in the beginning, the wound is invisible.

Edmond Jabés
The Book of Questions

PART 1

To the others, these accounts are about (one more) distant land,
like (any other) distant land, without any discernable features in the
narrative, (all the same) distant like any other ...Why resurrect it all
now. From the Past. History, the old wound. The past emotions all
over again. To confess to relive the same folly. To name it now so as
to not repeat history in oblivion.

Theresa Hak Kyung Cha
Dictee

There are many ways to fold a shirt.

It is important to fold it just right.

Fold it in half so a crease on the vertical
makes the wearer seem taller.

Fold it in half on the horizontal, then
in half again to form a square.

Fold it in thirds to fit nicely in a drawer.

Or not.

Remember to tuck in the sleeves.
Forgetting will bring a smile.

If the shirt is inside out, fold it as is.

Some shirts need ironing.

Sometimes I iron then fold.
Sometimes I fold then iron.

Sometimes I cry as I iron and fold.

I don't know why.

A glass of wine next to the iron helps.

When I began my study of crying,
I was not ironing. At age ten,
we are still folded.

The Catholic who would be Camelot
was talking on TV. All hair and smile,
he was someone for whom I would cry
though we had never met, someone
for whom I would try not to cry
because we had never met.

When the channel changed, I stood,
an empty glass of milk in my hand, my eyes
still on the TV—I saw

the arm of a backhoe, its hand,
fingering its way through a pile of sand, gathering
stones but they were not stones—I saw bodies
from an old war, their tattooed forearms flailing.
I saw them tumble like pretzels into a bowl.

Hair on the head moves us to tenderness.
Lockets of hair are saved for remembering.

Hair on a shoulder or chair offends—
on food, disgusts.

Hair can appear, disappear.
There is much to understand about hair.

The bodies—
bones with skin like rippled cellophane—
had no hair, shaved perhaps
or gone from disease.

The young ask questions about hair.

The young question everything
and understand early the silence
that swaddles the questions
they do not ask again.

I feel ironed, says Rose.
Look at my arm.

His neck droops
into the times
he has looked.

There is nothing, he says.

Not Jewish
nor German not
even sure
where Auschwitz is,
she reads her memories in ink
beneath the skin
of her left arm.

Dance with me, he says,
as if he has never felt
washed and wrung
and hung from a line.

She sees him then,
of percale, of 500 count,
in a one-two step
with the breeze. She longs
to run, to gather him
in her arms, to bury her face
in the smell of him,
the waltz of him.

I remember my mother
sorting towels from t-shirts, socks
from sheets. *Sorting*, she would say
when I asked what she was thinking,
sorting—not worsted wools from lily-
twilled cottons, not gentrified silks
from factory synthetics. She sorted
the difficult from the grays, the loud
from tired yellows.

I remember my mother in the yard,
hanging clothes on a catenary line—
one of the many things she simply
accepted. She would hang the ends
of two sheets with one clothespin
in a breeze, the sheets desperate
across her breasts, their ends flailing
at her hips—she a semaphore,
signaling.

In college, when I couldn't sleep,
I would ride in a dryer, think about silks,
about wrinkle and shrink. I would think
about my mother as perpendicular line to curve
and myself as round, as tumble—think
how laundry, from sorting to folding,
and especially the missing sock,
explains everything.

Last night I turned
to pour a glass of wine
and there again, the bodies.
All those years without rest, biding time
in the cycle of my remembering,
gathering like stones into a mound
in front of a backhoe,
tumbling into a hole.

I saw myself digging
through raveled arms and legs
to a time when I didn't know.

Don't be afraid. I must tell you what I saw,
so people will understand the crimes men do to men.
　　　　—Siamanto

Ruth stands on the corner of Washington and Main,
a black tulle veil on her head, a black cape
and gabardine slacks, her hands a cup
around a small sign—PEACE
—that seems to grow there.

Other women in black wing out from her,
their eyes lithe and present. People who pass
try not to notice.

They part as I enter. The weave of their silence
gentles my fall. I stand with them, listening,
a witness to my own absence.

Ruth goes deep into the fold of remembering,
her lips move, she thinks she is in a Greek play,
part of the chorus, one of the ones who always survives
to tell what she has seen.

She moans, she is sound, she is
the cry of wild before the human tongue
found the words to tame it.

She shifts her weight, lifts, extends her foot
and dances in her mind—a dance
older than Darfur, older than Iraq, older than
the Western Sahara of Morocco, older than Auschwitz
and older than Armenia, she moans and asks,
though she does not know who to ask, how—
How can I dig out my eyes?

Allied photographers in 1945
filmed the liberation of Dachau
and other camps. The films were shown
at the Nuremberg trials.

The ability of the human eye to see
and feel is an amazing thing. The ability
of the human eye to see and not feel
is an amazing thing. The ability
of the human eye to not see but feel is
an amazing thing.

It is good to watch movies on TV while ironing
but not a good thing while folding.

Little folding gets done while watching TV.

But some movies are not movies.
Some movies are not TV.
Some movies are something else.

Judgment at Nuremberg is not a movie.
It is something else. It makes you stand
hours with your glass empty,
your mind folding.

Ernst Janning of the Third Reich,
on trial in the movie, really someone
named Franz, really Burt Lancaster,

has as much hair as Spencer Tracy
and a resemblance in the eyes. He says,
Why did we sit silent? Why did we take part?

(Sometimes like children, we ask
when we already know the answers.) He says,

Because we were young, and we loved our country.
Because we were no longer young, and we were afraid.
Because we were old and understood everything
as a passing phase.

Some people cry when they hear these words.
But they are only the words of an actor.
They are only words in a movie, an old movie,
a repeat on late-night TV.

Yet people always cry. They cry without knowing why.
They cry because they are good people. They want to
forgive Burt Lancaster, a face familiar, yet unfamiliar,
someone they know.

I say it is only a movie, only an actor, only words
biding time in the cycle of our remembering, gathering
like stones into a mound in front of a backhoe,
tumbling into a hole.

Ruth opens her eyes, she sees
at the sidewalk café a man, gazing
up, counting. She goes, even though
she does not know how she goes, and
asks, Why are you counting the stars?

Five million one, five million
two ... If I count them,
they are mine.

That is rather poetic.
And what are you doing now?

I am counting the dead ...
Acadia: two, three, six ... Afghanistan:
one, four, five ... Belarus: two, three,
ten ... the Belgian Congo ... Bosnia,
Burundi: ten, eleven, twelve ...
Cambodia ... Darfur: two, six, seven
... Gaza: three, four, five ... Ghana:
four, eight, ten ... Guatemala ...

O! and Armenia ...

Armenia?

It was long ago but no one
has counted them yet.

Why are you counting the dead?

For you.

But you are of no use
to the stars, and I am of no
use to the dead.

five, six, seven … Iraq: six, eight,
nine … Israel: one, two, five …
Palestine: two, four, seven …
Tasmania, Tibet, Tokugawa …

When I was young, I ironed
two or three times each week.
Four shirts, two skirts—six
times four a month. Twenty-
four times twelve times three
years in high school. Two
hundred eighty-eight times
three: eight hundred sixty-four
pieces of clothing I ironed
as I stared out at the stars
through a window on the back
porch, counting. My father sat
at the kitchen table, reading
the paper, tallying the dead
in Vietnam. I iron little
these days. Maybe twice,
maybe three times a year.
My father is dead. Things
change. Things do not change.

Robert, living now in Mexico,
learning Spanish and married
to a Mexican woman who speaks
only Spanish, was a guard in Nuremberg
at the 1948 trials.

He was not in the movie.
He is in the movie I remember.

His gaze is not like that of the judge,
of Spencer Tracy, whose eyes fall slant
at the corners with the weight of seeing.

I wanted to ask Robert about the bodies,
about hair and the eyes of the judge.
I wanted to ask

how the witnesses walked to the stand—
if one toyed with his tie, if another
smoothed back a stray hair.

(Sometimes like children, the old
ask questions about hair and other things
as they sip wine.)

Did they speak soft or loud? Sit with straight backs?
Did their bodies seem to fold with remembering?

He said, There is nothing to tell.
It was only an assignment.
A lot was in German. I didn't
wear earphones. They didn't translate.
It was a long time ago. I forget.

Munich, 1990. Charlie, a lifer
in the Army, and I washed clothes
while his wife and my husband
watched a parade.

He said he preferred to fold
his own shirts. He said
the Army has perfected the art
of folding.

He is a good man, he laughed
at his joke about folding.

Eager with plans
to visit Dachau, we left behind
a pile of clothes, unfolded.

Dachau from afar: dirt and concrete
and buildings built for dolls.

I looked up through chain-link fence
to the barbed wire, to the perched guard-
station, oddly empty. Bodies

appeared on the compound,
cellophane bodies, naked and
amorphous as heat waves. Hairless.

Fingers poked through
my side of the fence. They
hung limply at the first joint, absent
of even the thought of wanting. I said
I didn't know, I wasn't born—
how could I know? I looked away,

looked up, saw
solemn men—their guns
pointing at the specters below.

The compound filled. I walked
among them, the odor of attic.
Diaphanous beings, they passed
through me. I entered

a building where they slept, I lay
between them in their bunks, closed
my eyes, felt myself
falling.

I did not ask how they lost their hair.
I told them I remember.

Elfriede, 84, visits the double gravestone
at Eternal Home Cemetery, the Star of David
over the name of her husband, Fred, and her own,
though she is not dead and she is not Jewish.

They lived modestly in an apartment
in San Francisco. She gave to Jewish charities.
They walked the streets, her arm in his, with joy
and pride and elegant dress. They sang in German.
Between notes, she forgot her secret.

Elfriede, 23, married Fred, a Holocaust survivor.
Fred married a prison guard, though he never knew.
He knows now, she thinks—she wants to die.
She sees his pain unfold—she wants not to die.

Elfriede and her dog patrolled the slave-labor camp
for women at Ravensbrück. I had no contact
with any prisoner, she swears. But she remembers
every one. They visit her. *Sieh mich! See me!*
All the ones she saw without seeing.

She remembers the young ones—her age—and
the old ones who told the stories she heard again
from Fred. She remembers the one who spoke
to the ground. When the Nazis fled like roaches
in '45, Elfriede waited a moment behind.
She mouthed *verzeihen Sie mir*—forgive me.

The Justice Department has discovered Elfriede's
secret. They will send her back to Germany, to a time
sixty years ago. "I thought they might forget," she says
in final words to Fred. "I thought they might forgive."

I sit with Fred. He says they would sing
German songs. His voice lilts with the memory
of Elfriede, how she'd raise the hem of her skirt
ever so slightly, and they would dance.

All stories are about ironing
and folding. Life offers
many lessons in one, too few
in the other. In the practice of folding,
we fall, we skin our knees.

Rose came to Camelot by marriage.
She did not say she suffered, she said
when a person gets old, she remembers
how easy it is to iron, how hard it is
to fold. Time does not heal all wounds,
she said. The mind protects them
with scars—*the pain lessens.*
But it is never gone.

Kaiya is a master in origami.

She makes paper of kozo fibers
from the mulberry tree. With fingers deft
as the dance of a butterfly, she folds
an envelope, its paper translucent,
strong and absorbent.

People, she says, need a place
to keep their tears.

I think of Greta,
who lost everyone in the war.
She would shake her fist in the air,
her head bowed into the closing
cusp of her life. She would cry.

Near the end, with care but understanding
little, they peeled open her hand, one
finger at a time, her stare blank
with forgetting.

Specious scabs appear on the news,
on the radio—covering old wounds,
raw and waiting. Call me Rose. Call me
Greta. I listen with a pained ear, I pick,
I read with a festering eye.

I dream of a Jew
with an aquiline nose, a light
in her hand, blinding.

Emma, I say.
Aliyah! she cries.

I say, I am not a Jew. She says,
And I am not real, I cannot speak,
I hold no light.

I say, Call me Ruth. Call me Greta,
lost in the old, dreaming of new.
You may even call me Rose.
Today call me Emma.

I say, Give me your tired, your
homeless, your Jews, weary
from the fight.

I cannot see you, Emma calls,
lift that light and speak
so I can hear you!

Give me your wretched, your
broken, your ironed and folded,
ready to end the fight.

When I awaken, I remember
the words. I remember the torch,
the flame of imprisoned lightning.

I remember a poet named Emma.
I remember it was I.

It is unknown how many people cry in their sleep.

A victim of sleep terror awakens abruptly.
The fold of my scream accepts no comfort.
Sweating, heavy breathing, a rapid heart rate
suggest intense fear.

There is no recollection of the incident.

All those years ago, Aunt Esther was not waiting
for a train behind the Beaux Arts column

at Michigan Central. She'd watch the light crawl
through the arched wall of glass, stretch

and linger. A woman, all bone and crook,
would cross the marble floor like a mantis,

her hands clasped and leading the way.
Sieh mich? See me? she said one day to the floor,

to the fingering light. She shuffled as if her ankles
were bound. Her left shoulder rose as if

to listen. Aren't you clever, she said to Aunt Esther,
I see you have gotten away. Aunt Esther

became shadow to the woman. She clutched the cuffs
of her sleeves, hitched her gait. She shrugged

to perfect the art. They talked to the floor, they
walked to the trains, and practiced walking away.

We gather clothes from the line
as Aunt Esther tells this story.

My question slips within a sheet
as it sloughs beyond her grasp to mine.

Aunt Esther lifts the basket of clothes.
We seek out the sun for a place to fold them.

When I die and it is time to decide
the fate of my soul, I will stand before someone
with eyes like those of Spencer Tracy.

He will say guilty and send me away.
I will wait in the bar and have a drink
with the ninety-nine condemned in the trials.

We will watch their movie.

They will shout out the lines, act out
the parts—another *Rocky Horror
Picture Show*. I will sit with Franz
who asks to be called Ernst. I will ask him
if Spencer Tracy can ever forgive us.
He will say he already has.

To celebrate, I will order a round of drinks
for everyone. We will drink and we will wait,
intoxicated, unfolded.

There is something about a woman named Rose.
Still, rhizome, her memories slip like petals to her lips.

As a mother plants along a white picket fence,
how can she know the fate of her seeds?

In another dream, I am sitting
with Ernst at a table for two. He confesses
he is not Ernst, not Burt. I look again and see
no weight in his face, no fold in his eyes.
His face on fast forward changes with fury
to men long ago, to men today—men I
hate, men I have loved.

I order a drink and Spencer Tracy arrives
with two shots on a tray. Not Ernst Not
Burt says, There is a fever over the land.
Above all, there is fear. Fear of today, fear
of tomorrow, fear of our neighbors, and fear
of ourselves. I say, You said those words
in the movie. He says, That wasn't me.
He throws back a shot of whiskey. He says,
Why do we sit silent? Why do we take part? I say,
Because we love our country. He smiles.

We've seen the movie more than once.
We know all the lines. We order more drinks.

I tell a friend I dream
about a drop of milk at the bottom of a glass.
She dreams she is bald, dreams she is hair.
In another dream I am the Tin Man,
my chest full of empty. I am Alice, falling
down a hole—I say, I drink whiskey
with Nazis. She says she dines often
with an important judge. She looks
a little like Marlene Dietrich. In my dream,
she's Japanese. She says she can fold
a napkin into anything I please. I call her
Kaiya, though she is not Kaiya, not Ernst not
Burt. She tells me to pull back the curtain
so we might speak to the wizard. I tell her I dream
it is Spencer Tracy.

At age ten I began my study
of crying. All those years without rest,
biding time in the cycle
of my remembering, trying
to forget. Crying and not crying.
I want to click my heels and go home
to a time before the channel changed.
I want to believe in Camelot, in forgetting,
and a god who forgives my forgetting.

Sometimes I quit the ironing, drink
the last drop from my glass and stand
long moments, thinking about folding.
I stumble upon the knowing of my crying
and not crying. I fall and fold, I tumble
into the light of diaphanous forms
that say they can teach me the art
of forgiveness. Crescent, closing, Greta
pulls the curtain. I ask the questions
I asked as a child. I order another round
and make a toast: To the human eye.
It is an amazing thing.

There's no name for us
when the stranger stumbles upon himself in the stranger!

Mahmoud Darwish
The Butterfly's Burden

PART II

In Jerusalem, hope springs eternal. Hope is like a faithful dog.
Sometimes she runs ahead of me to check the future to check it out,
and then I call her: Hope, Hope, come here, and she comes to me.
I pet her, she eats out of my hand. And sometimes she stays behind,
near some other hope, maybe to sniff out whatever was. Then I call
her my Despair, I call out to her: Hey, my little Despair, come here,
and she comes and snuggles up, and again I call her Hope.

Yehuda Amichai
Open Closed Open

Some people iron.
Some prefer to fold.

My father would stand in the doorway
where the air was thin with the weight of him.

Some things I remember by their press upon my eyes,
some by the way they fold upon themselves.

My mother was a woman of silken thread,
a perfect crease on the vertical, her sides unaligned.

She was not *fold* but the trying.

As she packed her bags, I asked, Are you going?
She said, I'm tired.

Did I ever see her iron? Ever see him fold?

Today I feel safe beneath the lintel of doorways.
The packing of bags feels little like folding.

As a child, I brought home
what my father called strays
or *other*. My mother would sigh,
but even she thought red had no place
within the pale of our décor.
Only potatoes and parsnips were
vegetables. The only spice was salt.

The face of John F. Kennedy on my wall.
A scapular around my neck, promising
salvation. Chaim Potok on my shelves.
In a former life, I was a Jew.

On my door I hung: *Do not enter
this doorway.* When my parents
were away, I stood half in my room,
half out. I felt light, I took deep breaths.
I talked—to no one in particular. I
danced in red socks.

Well past fifty, I shed my first tear
for an Arab. Sulaiman Khatib
was not looking for tears.
I do not know where
he was looking. My mirror says
it was not my face, not my dress
nor sweater. It was not my hands
nor the way I sat, listening. Two days
have passed. He says he saw my words.
His eyes are finer than mine. I cannot
see my words. I am looking.

To the Promised Land—*aliyah?*
Yes and no. To Israel, to Palestine.
Bring an extra suitcase for your words,
he said. But beware and rejoice—
they may or may not pass the checkpoints,
pass customs. The wounded who sit
with the loneliness of a wall can see your words.
They will feel a duty to take them.

I hear stories like knocking
on the other side of my wall.
It is an old knocking.

At a restaurant, a man
at the next table speaks
with a young child in Hebrew.
He calls her Esther. I look
at him, he is looking at me.
He speaks to Esther, he
speaks in English. He is
looking at me.

Esther says to him—
or is it to me?—
You will really bring voices
from the other side? Why do I
hear Arab music? Arab voices?

It is an old knocking.

You hear about the going.
You think about going.
Sometimes you go.

Then you are there

between the ones who are
always there, between
where is the line
and the first fold.

Between is hard less hard
than going.

Jerusalem, you have changed.
Worry hangs beneath your eyes.
You have put on weight.
Remember?
We met in church.
Your truths still pray
within the folds of my skirt.

Knowing I am lost,
I climb down the tree,
pause for a touch to the bark.
I bear the grit as I worm the dirt,
spoon along the roots
to find the seed.

Something about the wind assumes
we are listening. A wandering Jew
makes its way up the trunk
of a pomegranate tree. It is wrapped
around a lone branch, extending east.
It lifts and exhales against the bough,
gently knocking.

Anita of Brooklyn heard the call—*aliyah*!
She speaks of celery, how it grew in empty soil
in the bloc of Gush Katif. She speaks of how
things were, the glass houses of peppers, eggplant,
and herbs of every kind, of her *dunams*, two acres.
She speaks of Aviel, her son, of his gift to Rabin—
tomatoes, their first, when he was three, she sighs
and remembers the leaving. She speaks of *emunah*,
of faith in seeds. She speaks of one last crop.

Maha of Libya listens. Remembers. She carries
through life the words of her mother, her father,
who were cast from their Ramle home.

She hears their words as moans.
They are hers—no less than brown eyes,
a long neck. When she was a child, their words
fell like wet stones from the sky. She hid
from the weight of their falling. When the skies
cleared with silence, she would gather the stones
where they lay scattered, carry them in her pocket,
raise one to the light. Study every side, as if a prism,
cry her parents' tears.

With the years, the stones became many.
Her mother would slip like a leaf from its branch
into the shadows: A Jew, she would sigh,
lives in our home.

Light, as it will, breaks through a cloud
to a stage of two—a cedar and a crow,
a thistle and a toad.

Anita of Gush Katif speaks.
Maha listens through the bones of her mother
and for a moment is not her mother. She says,
How sad to be forced from your home.

Anita cocks her head, looks long
into dark eyes. A stone falls from her pocket.

Maha picks it up, turns it in the light.

Eyes bully their way,
while ears have a gracious way
about them. They sit quietly,
fold into the waves of the unnoticed.

A cat, Ahmad says, is content
to forget about birds, to sit near the fire,
to brush your leg, warm your lap.
But store it in a box with no food, no
water, no room to roam, when you raise
the lid, it will scratch you.

Never again will it grace
your lap nor give arch and lean
to your presence. With a sigh, you decide
such a cat cares little for others. How vacant,
you say, how unpracticed in reason.

You urge it to accept your words,
your ways: *Even mice deserve a say.*

Eyes suck you in like darkness.
A low hum responds.

It yawns and springs in a vertical leap
to the top of the bureau. You do not
understand. It does not explain.

i.
Why is there a wall, *Ima?*
To keep out the Other.

ii.
I ask an old man, walking
along the wall, Where is the Other?

He speaks of white alliums.

I ask him to point the way.

When I cry it is too far
from the way I came, he nods
and sends me away.

Hagit hands us paper. I take blue.
It is thin like a pale sky. She will
remind some, teach others, how to fold.

I think of Kaiya. I remember
someone saying, I remember it was me,
that paper will not hold anyone's tears.

I talk to the children about peace,
says Hagit, as we fold cranes.
The wall laughs—what does a Jew know
about cranes, about peace?

Hagit stands to answer.
A woman wise in the art of folding
taught me, she says. A woman named Kaiya.

I drop my crane. It unfolds.
Thinking of Kaiya, I fold it again.

I have never seen a whooping crane
though others have and others say
I have

yet when I sleep
I lay my face upon a feathered back,
lift my arms, they lift again.

I have never been to the marshes
of Kushiro, have never seen their cranes,
yet *ori* I fold—*gami*, of paper
thin yet strong,

my fingers far older than twelve
and ill with war,
my woe as red as the brow of the crane,
who tells me we are dying.

I am Sadako, I fold
six hundred forty-four now
six more by night

even though
I'm so unsure
one more crane
or a thousand cranes—
even a thousand cranes
—even a thousand

Words invite across thin ice.
Shalom, they say, their words a rope.
They call you Jew, they call you other.
They buzz from trees, they swarm like bees.

Shalom, they say, their words a rope.
Teeth of buzz and tongue of wing.
They buzz from trees, they swarm like bees.
To break the ice lets in the cold.

Teeth of buzz and tongue of wing.
How short our reach and strong the pull.
To break the ice lets in the cold.
Wings and rope, they rise and fall.

How short our reach and strong the pull.
Buzz and word is all we've got.
Wings and rope, they rise and fall.
Who is other, who is not?

Buzz and word is all we've got.
They call you Jew, they call you other.
Who is other, who is not?
Words invite across thin ice.

A bird strikes the glass where we sit, gazing,
then lies aground as the cat at the window glares.

The dogs in the yard near and we run, our hands
cupped, as if we believe what we touch we can heal.

Do we cry for the bird or a memory
of our own bent wings?

The pain of a place or event slips into a crowd—
drifts, rises, reaches its peak on different breaths—
waits, and breaks of its own weight.

Abu George sits at the window of his home, his hotel,
staring out at the wall that killed his father, took
his land, broke his business.

He of rich brew, the *qahwa* in his cup, breathes
deeply, smiles. Each morning, he says, I awaken
and laugh to begin my day. What good does it do
to be sad? To be angry?

A belief in answers is a kind of hope.

I peer into the box from which everything
else has escaped and see the two lying there,

spooning. All my life I have watched
the turn of one into the other, my
roundness full of aching. Today

my eye lingers upon the angular lift
of the lid, both open and closed, its lines
asking then angling away, waiting.

In the quiet of Galilee, she can hear the sigh
of thousands of years.

Fields of olives line the road. The yellow of bananas
and sunflowers runs up the hills to the forests of pine and fir.
The city of Tzfat slips away in the mirror behind her.
A spider clings to the windshield.

Israel is the safest place in the world. Israel is safe …
the safest … in the world. She knows these words
like she knows any prayer.

Black patches darken the hills
where rockets from the north have wandered.

She stares past the spider to a sullen sky
filling with smoke from the fires on Mount Moran.
She slows the car. Considers going back.
The spider moves.

She wonders at its legs, their finesse when they weave,
their strength against wind.

Her ears pound in the silence. The car fills with the sweat
of ten families in the shelter of one room. A breeze
coming and going through the open windows
argues with hairs at her cheek. The spider inches
across the glass.

Last night was Shabbat. The children stood, as if
they knew. Rockets flew by like birds. One struck
nearby. Shrapnel ripped through the far side of the house.
Ambulances screamed.

A soldier, on his way to Lebanon, took her arm, a teacher
named Rhonda slipped through the other. They entered
the streets. Arm in arm, the people of Tzfat folded
into one another. Their murmurs of *safe ... the safest ...
and chai—we live!*—swayed with music.

They sang "Am Yisrael Chai," and they danced.

As rockets wing across the sky
into Israel for war, yet another war,
the voices of three thousand Americans call out
aliyah! and pack their bags for the promised land.

Baruch Ata Adonay, Eloheinu—
Blessed are you, our God. In the fold
of midnight, you listen to our prayers
bleed. I sing Tikkun Hatzot. You listen
as they listen. They are coming—there!
Is it two? I think two: young, one silent,
his eyes like full moons, and the other
all neck with a memory that swells
in the catch of his throat.

See how one covers an ear and cups
the other to listen. See how he falls
to the ground, says *Allah*. I, too, fall.
You touch his brow to raise him.
I lift only my head, see two moons,
hear a cry tumble from fractured lips.
The reckless aim of his knife
strikes below my heart. The boy
who tries but cannot clear his throat
pierces my neck. *Eloheinu*, my God,
see how he bathes in the flow of my blood.
He smiles and calls to you, and there you are,
listening.

My son is singing Kaddish at my funeral.
See how his head lilts to hear me sing
Tikkun Hatzot. And you, *Melech Ha-Olem*,
God of the Universe, there you are,
singing all the prayers you know.

The tide of fealty ebbs
from where you stand before us,
a white square on your head, a black cord
holding it in place. We wait in a quiet ripple
around you. Your head tilts slightly,
as if listening.

On the wall, a black-and-white
kaffiyeh and a face as familiar as any
on an American dollar—Abu Ammar, *father*
of Ammar. We called him simply Arafat,
gone this day two years.

You speak of ties to Hamas.
Your words, like the moon, rile the seas.

You speak of a drop of water, you say
it can dent the hardest of things.

You speak of the eyes of your son,
how the soldiers as clouds slipped in
with the night to arrest you. You speak
of what is good, what is right, for your people,
you—Abu, you, the mayor of Beit Ommar.

You say you cried,
though you are a man, cried for your son
that he learn of hate, learn of hard.

You know how the wound of a man
is passed down to his sons, to his people.
The man who can fold metes out no wounds.

I say you are rock, you are stone,
you are water. You say you are the moon.

I see how your moon can calm the seas.
I call you Abu in the art of seeing.
I call you poet.

What do I do with this man of Hamas
who is pleased, who smiles?

i.
Mothers crease their brows with concern.
They say want me to kiss it, want me
to make it all better?

Daughters learn: their mothers sneak
in the night, pick at the scabs, smile to see
their blood trickle, flow.

ii.
Sheira spends time with a prickly pear,
a *sabra*, whenever she can. Jewish pain,
she explains. Inside the flesh is soft,
sweet. Not even the cactus understands.
She points to its shallow cast of roots
ten feet away. She touches a spine.
She bleeds.

iii.
She holds a black-and-white photo
of Tovah and Chana, Y'chiel and Aaron,
the children of Moshe Mendel. She says,
doesn't say, see here are my wounds, my family,
of Poland, of Chorzele, *a shtetl*, a town,
where the Nazis held the first Jews.

She remembers at the knee of her mother
the story of two hundred Jews—
how they burned as other Jews danced
down the sight of Nazi guns.

She leans into her listening, hears Tovah
and Chana scream for their brothers.
Their blood flushes her cheeks.

I want to give her comfort, to find a scab,
let everything escape. I pick: perhaps
they were not in the synagogue, I say.
She say, You're right, perhaps instead
they died of hunger in Warsaw, in a ghetto,
or danced their last words in Auschwitz.

In the refugee camp of Al-Arroub,
birds wake you up. Smiles breach
the cracks of a wall.

The children play soccer
in the streets, without a ball.
They smell the bouquet of their gift,
as real as they imagine.

Their parents call them seeds.

A father still names his child
Bará, with hope she will grow up
innocent.

When the life of an Israeli son starts a war,
a father rethinks his life.

Free a thousand Palestinian prisoners if it will
bring home my son. Bring peace.

He speaks to everyone, even Hamas.
He seemed like a nice man, he says.

He grieves for the loss of twenty-nine Palestinians
in Beit Hanoun. He visits the wounded.

When a father looks for his son
inside a war, he finds himself.

He has visions of rockets boring through
the soil. Coming to rest, unexploded.

One day they will explode. They always explode.
Who listens when he shouts to his G-d *Enough*?

They gather in my room: the confused
and fractured. Sheira comes, the photo
she carries enlarged so all can see,
but only I see. She speaks in Yiddish
of Tovah and Chana, of Aaron, Y'chiel,
and yes he had a wife. Speaks too
of their father, though Sheira cannot speak
Yiddish, and says nothing of the photo.

I hear their names in her laugh, see their faces
in her eyes, feel them alive in the flush
of her cheeks, grieve them gone
in the trail of her sigh.

Kaiya shows Li-Young the paper she made
from a mulberry tree. With fingers deft
as the dance of a butterfly, she turns paper
into wings. But it is the poet who teaches
the Master about folding.

He speaks of the Eastern truth of time. Our lives,
he says, bleed through the memory of the past.
But what we see is already gone. Only sound
is real, only song. The possible, he adds,
and praise. He smiles, he says, I live in a hum,
in the quest for one note.

His lips round. He closes his eyes.
A fractured drone seeks its pitch.
Sheira leans to hear.

Pale, of Irish roots
and from America,
she tells the poet from Nazareth
she knows nothing of poetry.
He closes his eyes and recites,
Those that I fight I do not hate,
Those that I guard I do not love.
Yeats, she says, smiling.

She agrees with Jimmy that a line has been drawn
down the back of the country. Children hold hands
in a row, sing chants like Red Rover. They want to play,
they want someone to come over. Until a certain age,
children know if you trim a branch as it stretches
over the fence of your neighbor, if you cut away
trespassing roots, the tree will die. Then they forget.
They stand on their sides of the line because
that is what they do. But the times are without song.
They no longer hold hands.

Love at my side, *ahuva*, my beginning,
you stand guard at the wall of my dreams,
though you take long breaks, lose hours within
the center folds of magazines, peer through
cracks to the ways of *moti*, my death,
as she spoons around my sleep, lifts the silk
of my gown, exposing my thigh. A tongue,
reptilian, wet and forked, can reach the most
secret of places. The weight of you both is hot.
I close my eyes to one and the other sighs.
Love enters, I call out My *death*! In darkness
I rise up with the blue tip of a flame. In the light,
I slip away with an ache of wanting, a moment
of having. A memory of endings.

She played as a child beneath the lemon tree.
Her mother worried a lemon might fall, like the sun, from the sky
and everything would change.

Daughter, said she, you must love
neither land nor a tree
with faith it will always be.

Ima, she said, who planted our tree?
Her mother did not say.

With the years, she lay in the shade of the tree,
counting her suns. A mist some say sour, some
sweet, pierced the air when they struck the earth.
The juice slipped through a splintered rind, dry white
on her hands. She followed the lines, lost in the right
and left and return of their direction. She placed the suns
in a new orbit on the limbs of the tree. Like a god,
she was sure she could change everything.

There is an eleventh commandment,
said her mother: You must not change.

She was nineteen, it was spring, and time again to sing
to the tree. *Baruch Ata Adonay Eloheinu.* Blessed Lord,
bo're p'ri ha-etz, who creates the fruit of the trees.
Kneeling, her eyes closed and hands in prayer,
she swayed, her mouth round with praise,
as young Bashir watched at the gate.

It was not his cries that softened her song
but the pooling of milk and honey and wine
around her. His vowels held the air. She could not
breathe. *Allah,* he moaned, and *Tooba*—tree,
the tree of the Garden, the tree of life. She watched him:
a leaf of flow and fight in the wind. By way of his song,
she knew he came from the seed that planted her tree.

There is also a twelfth commandment,
her mother said, Thou shalt change. You will change.

We walk from the town to the wall.
A few olive trees. A few homes.

> Arab families in circles, their hands wrapped
> around glasses of tea, the cubes melting.

They look up as we pass. Nod.
They know the program.

> The sun glancing off the razor-wire fence
> along the road. A starling slips through.

Israeli soldiers at the wall. They laugh.
Wait for the games to begin.

> Bale wire divides them
> from the crowd, ready to unravel.

The media and crowd yawn with the waiting
for the wall to come down.

> Soon. Someone will cast a stone.
> A soldier will fire. The crowd, explode.

An Israeli woman, who refused Sharon's call
to war, stands watch at the checkpoint, the *machsom*.
A soldier bandies about an Arab farmer, shoves him
to the wall, spreads his legs with the barrel of a gun.
Pats him down.

Look there! the woman cries. It is your *ima*
who arrives. *Ima!* Come see your boy soldier.
Stand with us and watch him. He is a man.

We are different, she and I.

It comes to me—something—
as the sun glances off the leaves of an olive tree,
as the end to the call for afternoon prayer
returns quiet to the day, as boulders rest
on the lips of mountains
without thought of when they will fall—

it comes to me, how silent my step
across these ancient stones.

How odd of God to choose the Jews.
        —W. N. Ewer

Millions of birds linger in Galilee
on their way to Egypt. A crane rests on a branch
rising from the marsh. A spur-winged plover
in rabbinical dress calls out *did-he-do-it* and waits.
A jackal squints in the sun.

Carob and terebinth trees descend
the limestone hills of the Central Mountains
and disappear like ghosts into acacia and prickly sabra.

The wind carries what they remember, German
words from the camps of silence and hope—
ruhe! quiet! and *heimweh*, longing for home.
They remember thirst. Sleep is like standing
neck deep in water. When they bend their necks
to drink, it drains away.

It is a collective dream of eating. They lick their lips
and move their jaws as they sleep. They remember
figs and grapes. When they reach for the fruit,
the wind lifts the limbs beyond their reach.

Warum? they asked the guard. Why refuse
a dying man to cup his hands and drink the rain?
Hier ist kein warum.

Why? they are asked by men of the world
who have no thirst for a piece of land.
Passerines of song—the titmouse, swallow,
warbler, wagtail, and thrush will arrive tomorrow.
In spring, peonies will flush the northern mountains.
Vermilion lotus will bloom in the Negev.
There is no why here.

I remember the first war.
Before flint and metal and pictograph stone.
I see a woman in 2700 B.C.E. I notice it is me.
I am in the Middle East, my head bowed,
a clay pot and reed in hand. I am about
to write a word. One word. I see a mouth open.
It is mine. War!

For five thousand years—and how many more?—
a cry I cannot hold, the drop of my jaw,
the feel of a sound, a fistful of stones.

A lotus flower floats on her lower lip.
The notes of her cello form sprigs
between my toes. Holy, I say. *Heilig,*
she says and I fall. Pain has a life,
even in sound. The timbre of German
trumpets silenced truths. I remember
I am Nazi. I remember I am Jew.

I lie upon her bow
as it stretches across the strings.
Heilen, she says, it is time to heal.

i.
The leaves blink like brushed silver
in the flat light of Bi'lin on the West Bank.
It is late autumn. The olives are ready.
A bulldozer approaches. Asif weaves a chain
in and around his trees. It slips from his fingers
as the groan of an engine caterpillars over the ridge.
He attaches an iron collar to the end of the chain, snaps it
around his neck. It locks. He rests the back of his hand
to the bark of a tree like a man recalling his love.
The roots of twelve years are deep. What kind of a man—
even a Jew—can do this? he asks the tree, asks no one.
He sees it happen, the break of limb and root
as the machine rips it from the soil. He straightens
the scarf around his head, his *kaffiyeh*, his pride.
He leans into the tree, rib to rib, and waits.

ii.
Reuven looks to the lone tree on the hill.
It is two thousand years old. He still dips his bread
in the oil of its fruit. He remembers: *The Lord*
calls Israel a leafy olive tree. Jacob appears
over the hill, raising his ax. War! he calls out,
his smile unctuous, drooling. Reuven looks again
to the tree. During war, he says, men may besiege
a city, but may not destroy its trees. So is the word
of Moses. A man may eat of their fruit, but not

wield an ax against them. Jacob's eyes widen
with the knowing lift of an ax and the wind
of its fall. You forget, he cries, what they have done
to you, to Israel! Reuven sighs. The olive, he says,
is beaten and pressed. It bleeds oil. It rises up
not as ax but as glowing light.

Aman understands the walnut,
how the line of its equator,

like disconsolate lips, waits.
She understands the avocado,

sliced from point to round,
how one half falls away

from the pit. She misses it.
She is Muslim-Arab, she is

Israeli. She is a mismatched
sock after all the clothes

are folded. Solomon understands
the folly of splitting the baby.

So it says in Kings 3, in the Qur'an.
Aman is waiting for her mother

to cry out. My ear is pressed
to the belly of the land. I am

listening. Something stirs.
I feel it kick.

Some are a chosen few
who see the trees and understand
the forest. Elders and saplings gather around her.
Emma says every word planted, or given to the wind,
counts in the world we are trying to heal.

When a soldier of peace falls
in a battle against the wall of Bi'lin,
Esther forgets if it is she
or someone in her family tree
who is trained in the healing of wounds.

Leaves cross their own reflection
without any disturbance to the sunlit surface
of the lake. Elfriede does not look until a loon lands,
dives headfirst for food. Ripples arc the way a bullet
shatters glass. It is the fragments of things she understands.

Kaiya walks blond in the world
though her roots and her fire confess
she's a redhead. She crosses the world
to save it. Her ex and her children find her,
tell her they still do not forgive her.

Israeli soldiers detain Ruth
as she boards a plane for home.
It is her lips, plump with praise for olives
from the trees of Kamel Moghrabi
that betray her.

The pain we've seen is a bottomless pit—
how do we heal the wounds? Rose asks.
Salaam alaikum, she says to herself: Peace
be to you. *Shalom aleichem*, she answers.

i.
An olive hard and dark
on a gnarled bough, knows about flow.
The bark, with memory long before
Gethsemane, sings unguent tales.
Branches conduct with their lance-
shaped leaves. White flowers bloom
as they listen.

ii.
He is balsam in his touch,
the oil warm on his hands or
from his hands—it is hard to know.
Like the sweep of sea across
the shore, his touch wends its way
over the rise of bone, the ridges
of rib. I sink, as if through sand,
to a place ancient, rooted.

iii.
My love does not see the violence
in the breaking of egg, the sifting
of flour, the weight upon the yeast to rise,
the baking. He kneads the dough, feeling
only the moon's push of sea into sand.
He wipes his brow as heat and the escape
of yeast imbue the room, sighs as if
this is all he has ever known, this peace.

He fills a cup with oil, carries a bottle of red
from the cellar, lets it breathe. He looks out
upon the grove of trees now barren of fruit
and says, the things for which we wait
are the things that have always been:
wine, bread, oil.

iv.
The bread still too warm to slice, we break it.
We dip it in oil from—from where? he asks,
licking the drops that slip down his hand.
Israel, I read. *Mount Carmel*. Galilee—where
hope on faces is picked before it can ripen.
Produced by Jews, Arabs, Druze, and Bedouin,
working together. I saw this, I say. I remember
the hands, seeking an olive within the leaves,
like the weave of fingers through a lover's hair.

I believed in answers. I believed in Ruth,
Emma, Esther, Rose. I believed in the going
to Israel and Palestine.

But I have been there. I am not Ruth. I am not Emma
nor Esther. Not Rose. I am not. I am the why of the lift
of the bulldozer, the fall of the bodies. I am the why
of the flight of the Palestinians in '48 and the why today
of their fight. I am the why of the want of olive and home.
I am the why of war.

Paper and shirts understand folding.
They count the times they fold, knowing
their days are numbered. They fold and unfold
along the same crease. One day they break.

People and words understand little about folding.
They count the times they fold. It is not a difficult job.
It is light work. They have time for other things.
It is unclear why they break.

Notes

p. 20
Lance Corporal Hitler and the poet Siamanto
watched the Turkish genocide of the Armenians.
Hitler took detailed notes, thinking of Jews.
Siamanto wrote a poem, "The Dance":

> *I slammed my shutters,*
> *sat down next to my dead girl*
> *and asked: "How can I dig out my eyes?"*

p. 33
It has been said time heals all wounds. I do not agree.
The wounds remain. In time, the mind, protecting
its sanity, covers them with scar tissue and the pain
lessens. But it is never gone.   —Rose Kennedy

p. 36
The Jewish American poet Emma Lazarus dreamed of a home
for Jews in Palestine, years before the visionary of Zionism,
Theodor Herzl, published *The Jewish State*. A champion
of immigration to help East European Jews, Emma wrote
the poem "The New Colossus" to help fund the pedestal
for the Statue of Liberty. In 1903, years after Emma's death,
the New York arts patron, Georgina Schuyler, discovered
the sonnet tucked in a portfolio with other poems by her friend,
Emma. Schuyler made it her calling to have the last five lines
mounted on the pedestal:

> *Give me your tired, your poor,*
> *Your huddled masses yearning to breathe free,*
> *The wretched refuse of your teeming shore.*
> *Send these, the homeless, tempest-tost to me,*
> *I lift my lamp beside the golden door!*

Forty-two years later, the sonnet in its entirety was mounted
over the main entrance of the statue. In 1949, Irving Berlin
put the sonnet to music, sure the song would become the next
"God Bless America." It was a tribute to the statue or America
or maybe a tribute to Emma herself:

A mighty woman with a torch, whose flame
Is the imprisoned lightning, and her name
Mother of Exiles.

p. 53
Sulaiman Khatib: born in 1974 in the village of Hizme
near Jerusalem. A member of Fatah at age twelve.
In prison at age fourteen for stabbing Israeli soldiers.
A boy can learn things in prison. He attended classes.
A worker in the library, he studied English. He picked up
Hebrew from talking to his guards. He read. He says,
This is when I began having new thoughts. A boy can
learn a lot, think a lot in ten years and six months of prison.
Together with Palestinians and Israelis who wore well
the vestments of violence, he co-founded Combatants
for Peace, a movement of men who no longer believe
in violence as a means to resolve their conflicts.

p. 58
The prophet Mohammed said of his favorite fruit:
It purges the system of envy and hatred.
An old Arab proverb says: The pomegranate,
the *apple of many seeds* and true fruit of paradise,
contains one seed from heaven. It is best to not drop
a single seed, lest that seed be the one from heaven.

A compassionate listener asks, "What would the world
look like if adversaries listened to each other's humanity?"

p. 59
In 1948, with the establishment of the new Israeli State,
700,000 Arabs fled to Jordan and Syria, Lebanon and Egypt.
Libya. Maha's parents lost their home in Ramle, settled in Libya,
where Maha was born. When she returned home to Israel,
she checked the box *Palestinian* and settled in Haifa.

In 1967, Israel captured Gaza in the Six-Day War.
Anita Tucker came to Israel in 1969, started a family
farm in 1975. She grew celery and other plants in hothouses
on the sandy beaches of Gush Katif. During the Oslo Accords
in 1993, a timetable agreement was signed, giving much
of the Gaza Strip to a Palestinian Authority. Although
the Accords failed, Ariel Sharon ordered Israeli settlers
in 2005 to leave their homes in Gaza. We will sacrifice
land for peace, he said, with a unilateral disengagement
from the Strip by August 15. No, said Anita, in chorus
with other Israeli voices—*no*, no. Anita and her family
ended a way of life within a month.

p. 62
Ahmad Khieran, director of Al-Arroub,
the Palestinian refugee camp, wrote
to the Compassionate Listening delegates:

> *I would like to thank you for your visiting*
> *that's never forgotten. Next, I bear greetings*
> *from the families which they welcomed you all*
> *without any intentions. My dears, I am writing*
> *to you trustfully, and I hope we succeeded*
> *in making good and prosperous relationships*
> *that can make a better transformation. I believe*
> *that every one of us is able to build peace,*
> *justice, and equalities among all races.*

p. 63
Ima means *mother* in Hebrew.

p. 64
Hagit Ra'anan, an Israeli Jew, born in 1950.
By thirty-two, a survivor of war as child,
soldier, wife, mother. During the Lebanon War
of 1982, a Palestinian killed her husband.
She is a woman of many wounds.

Others call her a peacemaker. She says:

> *I don't think of myself that way. I don't*
> *think you can "make peace." It's already here.*
> *I just need to be that peace.*

She is a believer. She says those who can heal
the wounds of an individual can heal nations.
She carries the seeds. She plants peace poles
at homes and schools and businesses. Over seventy
now in Israel, in Palestine. She brings a pole, wooden
and painted white. Others decide how to experience it,
how to decorate it. How to be peace.

p. 65
Sadako Sasaki was two years old
when the U.S. dropped the bomb on Hiroshima
that early Monday morning, the 6th of August,
1945. At age eleven, Sadako, who loved to run,
was tired. Leukemia, said the doctors,
"the atom bomb" disease.

Her best friend remembered an old legend
about paper cranes, that anyone who folds a thousand
is granted a wish. Storyteller Eleanor Coerr writes
that Sadako folded only 644 of the thousand cranes

before she died. Her friends folded the rest
and buried them all in Sadako's grave.

Hagit folds, she teaches others to fold
as she tells the story of Sadako and her thousand
paper cranes. Sadako, she says, made the paper crane
an international symbol of peace.

p. 66
Delegates, practiced in compassionate listening, exit
a bus in Jerusalem. Arab boys shout out "Shalom,"
a Hebrew greeting for hello, for peace. The boys wait
with pebbles in hand, sure the expected echo
will confess the arrival of Jewish sympathizers.

p. 67
Markram El-Arja owns the Everest Hotel in Beit Jala,
near Jerusalem. The wall cuts off a way from the city
to his business. It blocked his way to enter Jerusalem
and take his father for medical care. The wall is almost
finished. It is coming. It will line the road to his hotel.
It will divide him from his land. It will be an end
to the last place where Jew and Arab can meet, share
a meal, talk over a cup of coffee.

p. 68
Leah Green, founder of the Compassionate Listening Project,
sits with Pandora's Box on her lap. All that is left, she says,
is compassionate listening.

p. 69
It began with a tunnel, six months in the making,
as Hamas soldiers dug their way to Kerem Shalom,
near the eastern edge of the Gaza Strip. In June
of 2006, they arrived. Two Israeli soldiers were killed.
A young corporal, Gilad Shalit, the first Israel soldier

captured since 1994, was taken. His worried father
was sipping coffee. How could he know
where the day would take him?

The next month, Hezbollah fired Katyusha rockets
into the northern villages of Israel and stole
two soldiers. Two more makes three.
Lebanon calls it the July War. Israel calls it
the Second Lebanon War.

Rhonda Tsipar, a New Jersey teacher, in Israel now
thirty-one years, has a rocket in her garden, waiting
to explode. Two sons went to war, a daughter
to the U.S. *A parent can give only so much of herself
to war.* A son returned with shrapnel in his jaw
and three millimeters from his spine.

When a rocket hit the Tzfat Hospital, Rhonda offered
her school as a bomb shelter to the maternity ward.
It is then she met Hagit, who told the story of Sadako.
Hagit taught the new mothers to fold peace cranes.

Such a small city to have so many names: Tzefat and Safed,
Safad and Zefat, founded by Noah's son after the flood.
The highest city in Israel, home to the first printing press
in the Middle East. One of the four holy cities of Israel
with Jerusalem, Hebron, and Tiberias. Home to Kabbala.

p. 71
The World Net Daily news reported on July 20, 2006
that during the war between Hezbollah and Israel,
"as rockets slam into Israel," three thousand Americans
immigrated to Israel.

p. 72
A code of Talmudic law says that every Jew should mourn
the loss of the temple that once stood on the Temple Mount

in Jerusalem. Every evening, Erez Levanon would recite
the Tikkun Hatzot, a prayer of healing and memory. He lived
in Bat Ayin, an Israeli settlement near Hebron, home to
a thousand religious-Zionist Jews. On the 24th of February,
2007, as he prayed in the forest near his home, two Arab boys
slashed his throat and stomach with knives.

p. 73
Mayor Farhan Alqam, a Hamas member,
elected to office in October of 2005, is mayor
of Beit Ommar, a town of 14,000 people
between Hebron and Bethlehem.

The father of two sons and two daughters, he is
also known as Abu Musa, *father of his eldest son,
Musa*. He is committed to nonviolence.
Are there other Hamas mayors who are advocates
of nonviolence? He replies, There are many—
in fact, most of them.

Beit Ommar is a farming community.
Thirty percent of its lands will be lost
to the encroaching wall. Sixty percent
of the threatened areas are agricultural,
says Alqam. He joined the farmers of his town
to harvest their crops. The Israelis were coming
to take the land. At 2 am, Thursday, August 24,
2006, Israeli soldiers surrounded the family home
and arrested the mayor. The children were sleeping,
but Alqam feared they would awaken and see
their father taken away. Mostly he feared
the experience would turn them bitter. After
fifteen days detention, Alqam was released.
He has been arrested many times
for "resisting the Occupation."

p. 75
It is written in Isaiah 56:5: *And to them will I give*
in my house and within my walls a memorial and a
name ("yad vashem") ... that shall not be cut off.

People bring photographs of their friends and family
to Yad Vashem, the Holocaust Martyrs and Heroes
Remembrance Authority, located on Har Hazikaron,
the Mount of Remembrance, in Jerusalem. Established
by the Knesset in 1953, it documents the history
of the Jewish people and the six million victims
during the Holocaust. Yad Vashem offers memorials,
museums, exhibits, and archives. There is a room,
round like the sky, with stars and no moon. A voice
utters a name. The stars flicker, fade, then reappear.
Out of the dark, another name.

p. 78
The Hamas spokesman for the Palestinian Authority,
Ghazi Hamad, listened gently to Noam Shalit, father
of the soldier son captured June 25, 2006, near Gaza.
Shalit says he is not political. He will meet with anyone
who is willing to speak with him about his son, Gilad.
He goes to Gaza to talk to more Hamas politicians, he
offers comfort to the bereaved who lost family and friends
during the "accidental" firing of Israeli tank shells
into the civilian homes of Beit Hanoun. He visits
the wounded who were evacuated to Israeli hospitals.
He tells them the violence must stop. To himself,
in his prayers, to the press, he confesses, We do not love
one another, but we are sick of wars and violence.

p. 79
Tod Marshall wants to understand the connection
of poetry and the possible. In 1996, he interviews poets,

collects them in a book, *Range of the Possible*. He interviews
Li-Young Lee, who talks about poetry as a quest, a longing.
Poets are in a dialogue with the universe, says Lee. If we fail
to realize this, then our poetry and our art is in jeopardy:

The poet is God.
The reader is God.

The writing and reading of a poem is an exercise
in mutual divinity. The creation of poetry, which is life
itself, is the practice of mantra ... the emptying of the mind
so that the thoughts that come are not various thoughts,
but all one thought—the universal.

A poem is a poem when poets are able to hit that one note.

p. 80
Taha Muhammad Ali quotes from the W.B. Yeats poem
"An Irish Airman Foresees His Death."

p. 81
Simon Schuster published Jimmy Carter's book *Palestine:*
Peace Not Apartheid in November 2006. The next month,
Carter wrote in the Opinion section of the Los Angeles Times
(Dec. 8):

With some degree of reluctance and some uncertainty
about the reception my book would receive, I used maps,
text and documents to describe the situation accurately
and to analyze the only possible path to peace: Israelis
and Palestinians living side by side within their own
internationally recognized boundaries ... The book
describes the abominable oppression and persecution
in the occupied Palestinian territories, with a rigid system
of required passes and strict segregation between
Palestine's citizens and Jewish settlers in the West Bank.

An enormous imprisonment wall is now under
construction, snaking through what is left of Palestine
to encompass more and more land for Israeli settlers.
In many ways, this is more oppressive than what
blacks lived under in South Africa during apartheid.

p. 82
The Arab people love poetry. They love Mahmoud Darwish
best of all. He could fill an auditorium of forty thousand
as he recited from *The Stranger's Bed*, poems about falling
in love with the other. How erotic, how disturbing, how
revolutionary, how normal: two strangers in bed, in
dialogue, in love. How exotic, how disturbing, how
revolutionary, how normal: two Hebrew words, *ahuva*
and *moti,* in a poem modeled after the poem of an Arab.

p. 83
The story of two families, one Muslim and one Jewish,
who lived at different times in the same house in Ramle,
is told in the 2006 best seller *The Lemon Tree* by Sandy Tolan.

Dalia Ashkenazi and Bashir Al-Khairi are central characters.
Bashir's father built the house in 1930 and planted
a lemon tree. In the 1948 diaspora, the Al-Khairis were
evacuated from their home. The Ashkenazis
and their infant daughter moved in.

In 1967, Bashir and Dalia began their friendship.
When her parents died, they left her the house.
She was torn by the love for her childhood home
and her understanding that Bashir felt the same.
More honorable than one family alone owning the house,
and more honorable than compromise, Bashir and Dalia
agree to turn the house into a school for Muslim and Jewish
and Arab Christian children. They call it Open House.

The Compassionate Listening delegation visited

the home of Dalia Ashkenazi Landau in Jerusalem
on Erev-Shabbat, the eve of the Sabbath. Maha El-Taji
shared with Dalia that Bashir Al-Khairi is a distant relative.
Mustafa Al-Khairi, she said, the mayor of Ramle
in *The Lemon Tree*, was her great-grandfather.

Maha spoke of the wounds carried by her father's family,
and therefore her father, about the past. Dalia wrote
a dedication to Tahsin Al-Taji, Maha's father, in a copy
of *The Lemon Tree*: "I hope you can forgive us."

The Israeli poet Yehuda Amichai writes in *Open Closed Open*:

I want to give him some advice: Listen, my son, don't change.

Remember: Thou art what thou art. On a hot day,
drink a lot of water—chug it down and change ...

I would like to add two more commandments to the ten:
the Eleventh Commandment, "Thou shalt not change,"
and the Twelfth Commandment, "Thou shalt change. You
will change."
My dead father added these for me.

p. 85
Every Friday since the summer of 2005,
in the Israeli-occupied Palestinian village of Bi'lin,
a protest is held against the encroaching separation wall
that cuts off much of the village's farmland. Israelis,
Palestinians, and activists from around the world
participate in the demonstration.

The protest begins in nonviolence.
Stone throwing and the unraveling
of the protective fence around the Israel soldiers
leads to a retaliation with tear gas, sound grenades,
live and rubber ammunition.

p. 86
Ronnee Jaeger, Adi Kuntsman, Yehudit Keshet,
committed to human rights, founded Machsom Watch
in January 2001. Today over four hundred Israeli women
stand with them at the checkpoints, demanding civil rights
for all civilians.

Shani Warner is a member of Machsom Watch.
She is a draft resister who wrote Prime Minister Sharon
a letter, in 2001, telling him she would not serve in the army.
Three hundred others signed her second letter. We refuse,
they said to serve in this war. Israelis, too, are responsible.
We refuse on the grounds of conscience.

The army is the focus of the Israeli society,
says Shani. When women have a baby boy, people say,
"Congratulations! You have a baby soldier."

p. 89
War is old, older than word. Writing appeared on stone or clay
as cuneiform in Sumeria, hieroglyphics in Egypt in 3100 BCE.
When Americans learn that the first recorded war was a battle
between Sumer, now Iraq, and Elam, now Iran, in 2700 BCE,
they nod with a knowing, not sure about that knowing.
War is old, older than word. Or maybe there was a time,
beyond myth and wish, we lived in peace.

p. 90
A classical cellist, lover of languages, and daughter
of a lecturer for Tibetan Buddhism, an American
of Chinese heritage and compassionate listener,
lives in Germany.

p. 91
The Arabs consider the olive tree a symbol of peace.
It is valued for its historical presence and its symbol

of rootedness to the land. Arab families depend on the olive
as a commercial crop and for their livelihood.
When Israelis uproot their olive trees,
they call this an act of war.

The Jews have historic connection to the olive tree.
The tree represents God's promise to Israel.
The tree represents the Word of God, the holy Root.
The wise men of the midrash in Jeremiah 11:16 state,
"The Lord called thy name (Israel) a leafy olive tree,
beautiful with goodly fruit." The midrash asks the reason
for the connection of Israel with the olive tree. Answer:
the people of Israel, however much they are oppressed,
cannot be destroyed. Instead, they will burn as light,
and shine on.

p. 94
Moghrabi's Olives, by Deborah Rohan Schlueter,
tells the story of Kamel Moghrabi, who flees Palestine
in 1948, leaving behind his land and olive groves.

Salaam alaikum is an Arabic greeting,
meaning "Peace be upon you." The same
greeting in Hebrew is *shalom aleichem.*

p. 115
The Dome of the Rock in Jerusalem, or the Temple Mount,
has significance for Muslims, Jews, and Christians.
Muslims believe that the rock in the center of the dome
is where Muhammad ascended to Allah in heaven.
They call it the Haram al-Sharif. Jews contend the site
is where Abraham was willing to sacrifice his son Isaac.
The Ark of the Covenant was placed in the first temple.
Mark 11 says Jesus prayed in the second temple, chased
the moneychangers from the courtyard, overturned their tables.
Matthew 24 says Jesus predicted the second destruction
of the temple. Only the Western Wall, the *Wailing Wall,*

the holiest place in Judaism, remains.

A chosen we, who gathered in Israel and Palestine,
now a forgotten moment in time. Some called them
an apple, each one a seed—she Muslim, he Sufi, she
Christian or Buddhist, religious or nonreligious Jew.
One with friends in Jordan or family in Haifa.
One remembers when she hated Jews. One lived
on a kibbutz, one loved a refugee.

Hand in hand they climbed to a holy place.
Some call it the Temple Mount, and others
Haram al-Sharif. When they asked, Wise One,
who am I? the answer was always the same:
You are tree. You are root.

سلام
שלום

ABOUT THE AUTHOR

Sarah Zale lives on the Olympic Peninsula in Washington State and teaches writing and poetry in Seattle.

LaVergne, TN USA
30 October 2010
202870LV00005B/1/P